BEYOND
SMOOTHIES

Project Editor: Lisa M. Tooker

Translator: Christie Tam

Editor: Michele A. Petro

Design & Typography: Elizabeth M. Watson

Layout & Production: Patty Holden

Photography & Recipes: Teubner Foodfoto JmbH

Printed in China

ISBN: 1-59637-027-0

CONTENTS

INTRODUCTION

SMOOTHIES

FAST, EASY, HEALTHY AND DELICIOUS!

An ideal food for health conscious, people-on-the-go, smoothies can be a wonderful breakfast, lunch, or snack. Fast, nutritious, and very easy to make, smoothies are blended drinks made from the combination of fruits, vegetables, juice, or other liquids, thickened with ingredients like ice, frozen yogurt, sherbet, or ice cream and flavored with a variety of seasonings.

GETTING STARTED

INGREDIENTS

As you will see from the recipes in this book, you can mix virtually any fruit, vegetable, and liquid to create smoothies with a wonderful variety of flavors and textures. About the only things limiting your options are your imagination and your palate. Here are some of the ingredients found in these recipes:

FRUITS: Apples, apricots, bananas, blackberries, blueberries, boysenberries, cantaloupes, cherries, coconuts, cranberries, dates, grapes, grapefruit, guava, honeydews, kiwis, lemons, limes, mangos, nectarines, oranges, papayas, passion fruit, peaches, pears, pineapples, plums, raspberries, strawberries, and watermelon.

VEGETABLES: Avocados, bell peppers, carrots, celery, cucumbers, onions, pumpkin, radishes, spinach, and tomatoes.

LIQUIDS: A variety of fruit and vegetable juices and nectars, buttermilk, coconut milk, coffee, cream, kefir (a slightly sour brew of fermented milk, often containing about 2.5% alcohol, similar in taste and texture to a liquid yogurt), milk, mineral water, soy milk, tea, and water.

BERRIES GALORE!

COFFEE TREATS

BANANARAMA

ENERGY BOOSTERS

ISLAND FLAVORS!

THICKENING AGENTS: Eggs, honey, ice, ice cream, sherbets, sorbets, tofu, and yogurt.

FLAVORING AGENTS: Cinnamon, cumin, curries, dill, garlic, ginger, herbs, honey, horseradish, liqueurs, mint, nutmeg, olive oil, paprika, parsley, salt, sugar or sugar substitutes, soy sauce, syrups, thyme, and vanilla.

As the list above shows, just about anything can go into a smoothie!

PREPARATION

Buy fresh fruits and vegetables when they are in season and at their freshest. Whenever possible, select ripe fruits and vegetables. Wash and peel these ingredients, remove any seeds if necessary, and cut them up into small, even-sized chunks. Put them in separate sealable baggies and throw them in the freezer. Your ingredients will always be handy for a quick smoothie whenever the mood strikes. Freezing your fruits and vegetables also helps ensure that your smoothie will be icy-cold and will thicken your smoothie without watering it down.

Another great tip is to make ice cubes out of flavored beverages like coffee or team and use these in your smoothie. When the ice cubes melt, they won't water down the beverage's flavor.

Finally, if you make more than you can drink, just pour the smoothie mixture into small paper cups and pop them into your freezer to create delicious frozen snacks that are great for hot summer days.

EQUIPMENT

The list of items needed to produce your own smoothies is short and sweet:

Sharp knife

Cutting board

Measuring cups and spoons

Spoon (for removing seeds)

Sealable baggies for storing and freezing ingredients

Blender or smoothie maker

BLENDERS VERSUS SMOOTHIE MAKERS

Any good quality blender with a powerful motor (700 watts or more) should do an excellent job for smoothies. However, specialized smoothie makers are also available. A smoothie maker often has a more powerful motor than the average blender and comes with extra sharp blades to easily crush fruit and ice. Our recommendation: buy a powerful blender from a top quality maker and leave the specialty machines to your neighborhood smoothie shop.

AND THE FRUIT JUST KEEPS ON COMING

DRINK YOUR FAVORITES

EXOTIC TASTES

TIP

▶ It is a good idea to weigh your bagged ingredients and label the baggies with the date, the baggie's contents, and their weight for easy reference. Try to use the contents within one to two weeks of freezing. If fresh ingredients are unavailable, you can often substitute packaged, frozen fruits or vegetables.

TOFU ANYONE?

BERRIES GALORE!

SWEET, CRISP, AND REFRESHING, berries are a wonderful ingredient for summer smoothies. These berry smoothies will lighten even the hottest days! And, remember, the vital nutrients in fruit help to keep you alert, aid in blood production, and help lower blood pressure, among a few, so you can never eat enough fruit—and smoothies are a great way to make it nutritious and fun.

Strawberry Zinger

1 pint basket ripe strawberries
3 cups cold milk
4 scoops strawberry ice cream
1 pinch freshly grated nutmeg
2 tbs sugar (amount as desired)
4 strawberries with stems
    for garnish
4 peppermint leaves for garnish

BRIEFLY RINSE strawberries. Set aside 4 strawberries with stems for garnish.

REMOVE STEMS from remaining strawberries and purée in a blender. Add milk, ice cream, nutmeg and sugar, and mix briefly.

POUR INTO 4 glasses and garnish each glass with 1 strawberry and 1 mint leaf.

SERVES 4

Strawberry Banana Smoothie

½ cup banana flesh, slightly frozen
1 half pint basket strawberries,
    cleaned and slightly frozen
⅔ cup plain low fat yogurt
¾ cup milk
2 banana slices for garnish
2 fresh mint leaves for garnish

IN A BLENDER, combine all the ingredients and blend very well.

POUR INTO A GLASS and garnish with banana slices and mint.

SERVES 1–2

Raspberry

Smoothie

2 half pint baskets fresh
     raspberries, cleaned
1 cup orange juice
     (about 2 oranges)
4 tbs honey
1 cup lemon-lime soda
     (e.g., 7UP or Sprite)
2 cups milk
1 pinch cinnamon
4 fresh raspberries for garnish

SET ASIDE 4 raspberries for garnish and purée remaining raspberries in a blender. Add remaining ingredients and mix thoroughly with a wire whisk.

POUR INTO 4 well-chilled glasses and garnish with raspberries.

SERVES 4

Raspberry Delight

1 half pint basket fresh raspberries
   (or 1 cup frozen)
2 tbs powdered sugar
1 tbs fresh-squeezed lemon juice
¾ cup vanilla yogurt
⅓ cup milk
5 tbs heavy cream

For the garnish
2 slices organic lemon
6 raspberries
Lemon balm or mint sprig

SORT FRESH RASPBERRIES and clean or thaw frozen raspberries, setting aside 6 berries for garnish. In a blender, combine raspberries, powdered sugar and lemon juice, and purée.

PUT RASPBERRY PURÉE through a fine strainer. Pour one-third into the glasses. Combine remaining purée with yogurt, milk and cream, and blend thoroughly. Pour raspberry yogurt mixture onto the raspberry purée.

FOR THE GARNISH: Cut halfway through lemon slices and twist into spirals. Arrange lemon slices, raspberries, and lemon balm leaves or mint sprigs on toothpicks and use to garnish drinks.

SERVES 1–2

Pink Berry

1 half pint basket strawberries,
   cleaned and slightly frozen
½ cup milk
1 dash lemon juice
2 tbs all fruit strawberry jam
¼ cup strawberry frozen yogurt
1 slice lemon for garnish
1 slice fresh mint leaf for garnish

IN A BLENDER, combine strawberries, milk, lemon juice and strawberry jam, and blend well. Add frozen yogurt and blend.

POUR INTO A GLASS and garnish with a slice of lemon and mint.

SERVES 1–2

Cranberry Smoothie

⅔ cup ice-cold kefir
¼ cup cranberry compote
(from a jar)
½ tsp floral honey
½ tbs lemon juice
½ cup vanilla ice cream
Dried sweetened cranberries
for garnish

IN A BLENDER, combine kefir, cranberry compote, honey and lemon juice, and blend. Then add ice cream and blend. Taste for sweetness and add additional honey if needed.

POUR INTO A GLASS and garnish with cranberries.

SERVES 1–2

TIP

▶ Kefir is produced from cow's milk. A slightly sour brew of fermented milk, kefir is similar in both taste and texture to a liquid yogurt. Many supermarkets carry kefir in the natural food section.

Spring Berries

1 cup strawberries, sliced
½ cup well-chilled plain yogurt
1 tsp lemon juice
1 tbs strawberry syrup
1 dash vanilla extract
⅓ cup strawberry ice cream
Mint leaves for garnish

CLEAN STRAWBERRIES, rinse, drain well, and slice.

IN A BLENDER, combine strawberries, yogurt, lemon juice, syrup and vanilla, and blend well. Add ice cream, blend, pour into a glass, and garnish with mint leaves.

SERVES 1–2

Red Angel

1 half pint basket red berries
    (e.g., raspberries, strawberries),
    cleaned and slightly frozen
½ cup cranberry juice
½ cup vanilla ice cream
Mint sprigs for garnish

IN A BLENDER, combine berries
and cranberry juice and gradually
blend in ice cream.

POUR INTO A GLASS and garnish
with mint.

SERVES 1–2

Blue Angel

1 cup blueberries, slightly frozen
½ cup well-chilled milk
1 tsp honey
1 dash lemon juice
½ cup blueberry frozen yogurt
    or ice cream
Blueberries for garnish (if desired)

IN A BLENDER, combine all the
ingredients, blend well, and pour
into a glass.

IF DESIRED, garnish with
whole blueberries.

COFFEE TREATS

THESE COFFEE-FLAVORED DRINKS will give you the boost you need for those action-packed days! You'll find these drinks provide your body with energy as well as the healthy nutrients it needs. It's also a great way to jump start your morning when you don't have time to fix a full breakfast.

Blue Mountain

½ cup cold Blue Mountain
    coffee (Jamaican coffee)
4 tsp heavy cream
1½ tbs cherry syrup
½ cup well-chilled milk
½ cup coffee ice cream
Instant coffee for sprinkling

IN A BLENDER, combine all
the ingredients and blend well.

POUR INTO A GLASS and
sprinkle with instant coffee.

SERVES 1–2

Mocha Delight

½ cup well-chilled milk
½ cup cold coffee
2 tbs Ovaltine
4 tsp coffee syrup
½ cup coffee ice cream
½ cup vanilla ice cream
Grated chocolate for garnish

IN A BLENDER, combine all
the ingredients and blend well.

POUR INTO A GLASS and
sprinkle with grated chocolate.

SERVES 1–2

Coffee Banana Smoothie

½ cup banana flesh, slightly frozen
1½ cups well-chilled milk
½ cup well-chilled coffee yogurt
½ tsp cinnamon
1 pinch nutmeg
Banana slices for garnish
Instant coffee for sprinkling

COMBINE ALL the ingredients in a blender and blend very well.

POUR INTO A GLASS and garnish banana slices and sprinkle with instant coffee.

SERVES 1–2

BANANARAMA

LOADED WITH VITAMINS and potassium, bananas are a smoothie favorite!

Chocolate Covered Banana

1 cup ice-cold milk
1 level tsp cocoa
Seeds from ½ vanilla bean
    (or 1 dash vanilla extract)
½ lb banana flesh, chopped
    and slightly frozen
1 tsp floral honey
½ cup chocolate ice cream
Several sliced almonds
    for garnish

IN A BLENDER, combine milk, cocoa, vanilla bean seeds, banana and honey, and blend. Add ice cream and blend.

POUR INTO A GLASS and sprinkle with sliced almonds for garnish.

SERVES 1–2

Frosty Fruit Smoothie

½ cup diced banana flesh,
    slightly frozen
½ cup cold apple juice
½ cup cold milk
1 dash vanilla extract
4–6 ice cubes
Apple wedges for garnish

IN A BLENDER, combine all the ingredients and blend thoroughly.

PLACE ICE CUBES in a glass, pour smoothie over the top, and garnish with apple wedges.

SERVES 1–2

Mixed Fruit Smoothie

½ cup banana flesh,
  slightly frozen
½ cup mango, diced
½ cup well-chilled vanilla
  soy yogurt
1 tsp floral honey
½ cup well-chilled soy milk
1 stalk lemon grass
Ground pistachios for garnish

IN A BLENDER, combine all the
ingredients, blend well and pour
into a glass.

INSERT LEMON GRASS stalk
and sprinkle with pistachios
for garnish.

SERVES 1–2

Banana Lemon Smoothie

2 bananas
2 cups milk
4 scoops lemon sherbet
Juice from 2 lemons
Artificial sweetener or sugar
    (amount as desired)
1 cup lemon-lime soda
    (e.g., 7UP or Sprite)
Grated chocolate for garnish

PEEL BANANAS and purée in a blender with milk. Combine lemon sherbet and lemon juice and add to banana milk. Sweeten with artificial sweetener or sugar as desired and add soda.

POUR INTO glasses and serve cold. Garnish tops with grated chocolate, if desired.

SERVES 1–2

ENERGY BOOSTERS

THESE SMOOTHIES ARE EXCELLENT for athletes or anyone craving an extra boost of energy during the day! They are the perfect choice for those that need a high supply of nutrients but don't want all the calories. Replenish your body with these great choices to fill you up in the morning or any time of day.

Peanut Butter Smoothie

2 tbs peanut butter
1 cup well-chilled milk
½ cup vanilla ice cream
1 dash vanilla extract
Tuille cookies (optional)
Grated chocolate for sprinkling
Mint leaves for garnish

IN A BLENDER, combine peanut butter and milk and blend well. Add vanilla ice cream and vanilla and blend.

POUR INTO A GLASS and serve with a thin, crisp buttery cookie, if desired. Sprinkle chocolate over top and garnish with mint leaves.

SERVES 1–2

TIP

▶ Instead of vanilla ice cream, you can also use chocolate ice cream.

Biker's Smoothie

½ cup banana flesh,
    slightly frozen
½ cup strawberries,
    slightly frozen
4 tsp banana syrup
    (or ½ tsp banana extract)
½ cup orange juice
½ cup milk
½ cup strawberry ice cream

IN A BLENDER, combine all the
ingredients, blend well, and pour
into a glass.

SERVES 1–2

Beta Boost

½ cup mango flesh, diced
1 half basket strawberries,
    cleaned and slightly frozen
1 pinch chile pepper, seeds
    removed and chopped
½ cup well-chilled carrot juice

IN A BLENDER, combine mango,
strawberries, carrot juice and chile
pepper, and blend well.

POUR INTO a glass.

SERVES 1–2

Wellness Cup

Carrot juice
1 cup cantaloupe flesh, slightly
    frozen and chopped
½ cup carrot juice
½ cup orange juice
½ cup plain low fat yogurt
1 dash vanilla extract

POUR CARROT JUICE into an ice cube tray and freeze overnight.

IN A BLENDER, combine all the ingredients and blend well.

PLACE CARROT JUICE ice cubes in a glass and pour drink over the top.

SERVES 1–2

Carrot Apple Smoothie

½ lb carrots
½ cup water
1½ cups apple juice
2–3 tbs crushed ice

PEEL CARROTS and chop. Place water and carrots in a saucepan, cover, and simmer until tender, adding a little water if necessary. Let carrots cool completely.

IN A BLENDER, combine carrots, cooking water and apple juice, and blend well.

PLACE CRUSHED ICE in a glass and pour smoothie over the top.

SERVES 1–2

Orange Buttermilk with Brewer's Yeast

2 organic oranges
2 pasteurized egg yolks
1 tbs brewer's yeast
2 tbs fresh-squeezed lemon juice
Grated peel from 1 organic lemon
1 cup buttermilk
2 orange wedges for garnish

RINSE ORANGES under hot water and dry. Cut in half and set aside 2 thin wedges for garnish. Squeeze juice from orange halves.

IN A BLENDER, combine egg yolks and brewer's yeast and blend.

ADD ORANGE JUICE, grated lemon peel, and buttermilk to the blender and blend well.

POUR INTO GLASSES and garnish with reserved orange wedges.

SERVES 2

Vitamin Smoothie

1 cup cantaloupe flesh, chopped
½ cup cucumber, peeled, seeded, and diced
½ lb seedless green grapes
½ cup white grape juice
Cantaloupe for garnish
Lettuce greens for garnish

SET ASIDE a few finely diced cantaloupe pieces for garnish. Freeze cantaloupe, cucumber, and grapes briefly.

IN A BLENDER, combine frozen ingredients and juice and blend well.

POUR INTO A GLASS and garnish with reserved cantaloupe pieces and lettuce greens.

SERVES 1–2

ISLAND FLAVORS!

PRETEND YOU'RE IN THE SOUTH SEAS with one of these light, refreshing tropical treats. You'll find tropical fruits are the best as well as fruits that are in season and fresh.

Many exotic fruit also supply valuable plant protein. In Southeast Asia, coconut is known to help with heartburn and gastritis—so the benefits are not only tasty but provide the body with an excellent source of minerals and vitamins.

Tropical Fruit
Smoothie

½ cup mango flesh, chopped
½ cup banana flesh, slightly
 frozen and chopped
½ lb strawberries, chopped
 and slightly frozen
1 cup ice-cold unsweetened
 coconut milk
4–6 ice cubes
Nasturtium flowers for garnish

IN A BLENDER, combine mango, banana, strawberries and coconut milk, and blend very well.

PLACE ICE CUBES in a glass, pour drink over the top, and garnish with a few nasturtium flowers.

SERVES 1–2

Fit for the Sun

½ cup strawberries, cleaned
½ cup mango, diced
½ cup banana, peeled and diced
½ cup guava nectar
½ cup banana ice cream
Mint leaves for garnish

IN A BLENDER, combine fruit, guava nectar and ice cream, and blend well.

POUR INTO A GLASS and garnish with a mint leaf.

SERVES 1–2

Blood Orange Drink

2 blood oranges
1 pink grapefruit
½ cup ice-cold black tea
    (Darjeeling or Earl Grey)
1 tsp maple syrup
2 tbs crushed ice
½ cup blood orange
    sorbet (optional)
Crushed ice

REMOVE THE CAP from the oranges and grapefruit. Using a small sharp knife, remove the peel from top to bottom in segments. Cut along inner membranes and remove segments. Squeeze juice from membranes onto the segments.

IN A BLENDER, combine segments, juice, tea, syrup and crushed ice, and blend well. If desired, blend in sorbet.

PLACE A LITTLE crushed ice in a glass and pour drink over the top.

SERVES 1–2

Sunshine

½ cup papaya, peeled and diced
½ cup fresh pineapple, diced
½ cup banana, peeled and diced
½ cup well-chilled milk
4 tsp pineapple syrup
Crushed ice

IN A BLENDER, combine all the
ingredients and blend well.

PLACE CRUSHED ICE in a glass,
pour drink over the top, and serve.

SERVES 1–2

Heartbreaker

½ cup cherry juice
½ cup passion fruit nectar
4 tsp banana syrup
½ cup plain low fat yogurt
½ cup vanilla ice cream

IN A BLENDER, combine all
the ingredients and blend well.

POUR INTO a glass and serve.

SERVES 1–2

Cocolada

4 tsp coconut syrup
4 tsp chocolate syrup
   (e.g., Hershey's)
1 cup well-chilled coconut milk
½ cup chocolate ice cream
Coconut shell, if desired

IN A BLENDER, combine all the ingredients, blend very well, and pour into a glass.

IF DESIRED, you can also serve in half a coconut shell with a straw.

SERVES 1–2

Hawaiian Holiday

½ lb pineapple flesh,
    slightly frozen
4 tsp strawberry syrup
4 tsp coconut syrup
½ cup ice-cold milk
½ cup pineapple juice
½ cup coconut ice cream

IN A BLENDER, combine all the ingredients and blend well.

POUR INTO A GLASS and serve.

SERVES 1–2

TIP

▶ Flavored syrups can often be found in the gourmet coffee section
of a specialty grocery store.

Tropical Breeze

½ cup well-chilled passion
   fruit nectar
½ cup well-chilled milk
4 tsp grenadine syrup
½ cup vanilla ice cream
Pomegranate seeds for garnish

IN A BLENDER, combine all the ingredients and blend well.

POUR INTO A GLASS and garnish with pomegranate seeds.

SERVES 1–2

Sweetie

½ cup pink grapefruit segments
½ cup mango, peeled and diced
4 tsp mango syrup
½ cup well-chilled buttermilk
Mango for garnish

IN A BLENDER, combine all
the ingredients and blend well.

POUR INTO A GLASS and
sprinkle over top with finely
diced mango for garnish.

SERVES 1–2

Cherry Coconut

½ lb cherries
½ cup well-chilled cherry juice
½ cup milk
½ cup cherry ice cream
1½ tbs coconut syrup
Grated coconut for garnish

REMOVE STEMS from cherries,
rinse, remove pits, and chop.

IN A BLENDER, combine all
the ingredients and blend well.

POUR INTO A GLASS and
sprinkle with grated coconut
for garnish.

SERVES 1–2

AND THE FRUIT JUST KEEPS ON COMING

TRY THESE WILD AND WONDERFUL fruit combinations to "juice" up your taste buds! They are not only healthy but also nourish your mind with natural fructose that provides steady levels of energy for the brain without putting stress on your blood sugar level.

Melon Apple Kiwi

1 small Granny Smith apple
½ lb kiwis
½ lb honeydew melon flesh
2 tbs sugar
1 tsp lime juice
6 tbs crushed ice
Mint sprigs for garnish

PEEL AND CORE apple. Peel and chop kiwis and briefly place apples, honeydew, and kiwis in the freezer until slightly frozen.

IN A BLENDER, combine fruit, sugar, lime juice and crushed ice, and blend very well.

POUR INTO A GLASS and garnish with mint.

SERVES 1–2

Tangerines

Strawberry syrup
Sugar
2 tangerines, peeled and
    separated into segments
½ cup fresh, well-chilled
    tangerine juice
1 tbs orange blossom honey
½ cup well-chilled milk
½ cup tangerine sorbet
1–2 kumquat
Mint leaves for garnish

DIP RIM OF GLASS in strawberry syrup and then in sugar.

IN A BLENDER, combine all the ingredients and blend thoroughly. Cut kumquat in half and place on a skewer for garnish. Pour into a glass and garnish with kumquat and mint leaves.

SERVES 1–2

Summer of Love

2 tbs strawberry syrup
½ cup cranberry juice
½ cup unsweetened pineapple juice
½ cup unsweetened coconut milk
Mint sprigs for garnish

IN A BLENDER, combine all the ingredients and blend very well.

POUR INTO A GLASS and garnish with mint.

SERVES 1–2

TIP

► Flavored syrups can often be found in the gourmet coffee section of a specialty grocery store.

Kiwi Kiss

½ lb kiwis
½ cup ice-cold milk
2 tbs Midori liqueur (optional)
½ cup lemon sherbet
1 dash lime juice
Lemon slices for garnish
Kiwi slices for garnish
Mint sprigs for garnish

PEEL KIWIS and chop and reserve
a few slices of kiwi for garnish.

IN A BLENDER, combine kiwis,
milk, liqueur, sherbet and lime
juice, and blend briefly.

POUR INTO A GLASS and
garnish with slices of lemon,
reserved kiwi, and mint sprigs.

SERVES 1–2

Super Mango Smoothie

½ lb mango flesh, slightly frozen
½ cup chilled mango nectar
½ cup plain low fat yogurt
1 tsp honey
1 pinch cardamom
Mango wedges for garnish

CHOP MANGO and reserve and slice a few wedges of mango for garnish. In a blender, combine all the ingredients and blend well.

POUR INTO A GLASS and garnish with reserved mango wedges.

SERVES 1–2

Apricot, Pineapple, and Strawberry Fruit Smoothie

½ cup pineapple flesh,
   finely chopped
½ cup apricot flesh,
   finely chopped
½ cup fresh strawberries,
   finely chopped
½ cup banana flesh,
   finely chopped
1½ cups ice-cold milk
½ cup frozen apricot yogurt
   or ice cream
Banana slices for garnish

RESERVE A FEW slices of banana for garnish and freeze fruit slightly.

IN A BLENDER, combine fruit, milk and ice cream, and blend well.

POUR INTO A GLASS and garnish with reserved banana slices.

SERVES 1–2

Pineapple Dream

½ cup pineapple flesh, slightly
    frozen and chopped
½ cup ice-cold milk
1 tsp honey
1 dash vanilla extract
1 tsp pineapple syrup
1 tsp lime juice
½ cup pineapple ice cream
    or sherbet
1 tbs crushed ice

IN A BLENDER, combine all the ingredients and blend well.

POUR INTO A GLASS and serve.

SERVES 1–2

White Peach Cocktail

3 white peaches
1½ cups milk
½ cup heavy cream
4–5 crushed ice cubes
1 cup lemon sorbet
Several peppermint leaves
    cut into strips

CUT A SHALLOW "X" on the bottom of each peach with a paring knife. Plunge peaches in boiling water for about a minute, then place into ice water, peel, cut in half, remove pits, and purée coarsely in a blender. Add milk, cream and crushed ice, and mix well.

PLACE 2–3 TABLESPOONS lemon sorbet in tall glasses. Pour peach mixture over the sorbet and garnish with peppermint.

SERVES 1–2

Yogurt Currant Smoothie

½ cup plain yogurt
½ cup ice-cold pink
    grapefruit juice
½ cup ice-cold milk
4 tsp cassis (black currant syrup)
½ cup raspberry or
    blackberry sorbet

IN A BLENDER, combine all the ingredients and blend very well.

POUR INTO A GLASS and serve.

SERVES 1–2

Happiness

½ cup cherry juice
6 oz sweet cherries
2 tsp lime juice
4 tsp cinnamon syrup
½ cup well-chilled buttermilk
Mint leaves for garnish

POUR CHERRY JUICE
into an ice cube tray and
freeze overnight.

REMOVE STEMS from
cherries, rinse, remove pits,
chop, and freeze slightly.

IN A BLENDER, combine
cherries, lime juice, syrup
and buttermilk, and blend
very well.

POUR INTO A GLASS, add
4–5 cherry ice cubes, and
garnish with mint leaves.

SERVES 1–2

DRINK YOUR VEGGIES

DON'T THINK THAT FRUITS SMOOTHIES are the only way to go—try these tasty veggie drinks and get a whole new twist on enjoying your vegetables.

You'll also find that your mood starts to improve with "happy messengers" from the protein and nutrients found in vegetables. Soon after enjoying a vegetable smoothie, your body will start producing more serotonin and endorphins—so drink up to good times!

Tomato Buttermilk Drink

3 cups buttermilk
2 cups tomato juice
½ cup heavy cream
½ cup brown sugar
½ tsp salt
1 tomato
1 tbs chopped parsley
Diced tomato for garnish
Diced parsley for garnish

IN A BLENDER, blend buttermilk, tomato juice, cream, sugar, and salt.

RINSE TOMATO, cut in half, squeeze out seeds, and dice finely.

POUR BUTTERMILK MIXTURE into 4 glasses, add ice cubes, if desired, and sprinkle with diced tomato and parsley.

SERVES 4

Tomato Carrot Drink

½ cup well-chilled tomato juice
½ tsp fresh ginger root
1 dash light soy sauce
1 tsp honey
½ cup well-chilled carrot juice

POUR TOMATO JUICE into
a glass.

PEEL GINGER and grate finely.

COMBINE GINGER, soy sauce,
honey and carrot juice, and pour
onto tomato juice.

SERVES 1–2

Tomatino

½ cup chilled tomato juice
½ cup chilled milk
1 tsp basil
1 pinch chopped chile pepper
Salt
Pepper
2–3 tbs crushed ice
Finely diced tomato for garnish
Finely diced basil for garnish

IN A BLENDER, combine all
the ingredients and blend well.

POUR INTO A GLASS and
garnish with tomato and basil.

SERVES 1–2

Tomato Avocado Medley

2 small tomatoes (about 10 oz)
½ cup avocado, diced
½ cup lemon yogurt
1½ tbs tomato paste
1 dash white balsamic vinegar
1 dash Tabasco Sauce
½ cup tomato juice
2 tbs crushed ice
Several rosemary blossoms
    for garnish

RINSE TOMATOES, cut into quarters, and remove cores and seeds. Make sure to seed tomatoes over a strainer and save the juice. Chop tomatoes.

IN A BLENDER, combine tomatoes, strained juice, avocado, yogurt, tomato paste, vinegar, Tabasco, tomato juice and ice, and blend well.

POUR INTO A GLASS and garnish with rosemary blossoms.

SERVES 1–2

Garden Vegetable Drink

1½ bunches radishes
½ onion
2 cups chilled kefir, separated
2 tbs lemon juice
Salt
Freshly ground white pepper

For the garnish
Lemon juice
Fresh parsley, finely chopped
2 radishes, finely chopped
Fresh chives, finely chopped
4 lemon slices
4 radish slices

RINSE RADISHES, remove stems, and chop coarsely. Peel onion and dice.

IN A BLENDER, combine onion, radishes, 1 cup of kefir and lemon juice. Blend thoroughly and then add remaining 1 cup of kefir. Season to taste with salt and pepper.

DIP THE RIMS of 4 tall glasses in lemon juice, then in parsley. Pour in radish drink, sprinkle with radishes, and a few chives. Place 1 lemon slice and 1 radish slice on the rim of each glass.

SERVES 4

TIP

▶ Kefir is produced from cow's milk. A slightly sour brew of fermented milk, kefir is similar in both taste and texture to a liquid yogurt. Many supermarkets carry kefir in the natural food section.

Bugs Bunny

½ cup carrot juice
1 tsp chopped herbs
   (e.g., parsley, thyme)
½ cup cold kefir
Salt
Pepper
Grated carrot for garnish
Sliced cherry tomatoes for garnish
Thyme sprigs for garnish
Thyme leaves for garnish

IN A BLENDER, combine carrot juice, herbs, kefir, salt and pepper, and blend very well.

POUR INTO A GLASS and garnish with grated carrot, tomato slices, thyme leaves, and thyme sprigs.

SERVES 1–2

TIP

▶ Kefir is produced from cow's milk. A slightly sour brew of fermented milk, kefir is similar in both taste and texture to a liquid yogurt. Many supermarkets carry kefir in the natural food section.

Carrot Shake

1 tsp chopped parsley
1 tsp olive oil
½ cup carrot juice
½ cup plain soy yogurt
1 pinch ground cumin
1 dash lime juice
A little sea salt (optional)
Carrot stick for garnish

PLACE PARSLEY and olive oil in a mortar and pulverize, setting aside.

IN A BLENDER, combine carrot juice, yogurt, cumin, lime juice and salt, and blend well.

POUR INTO A GLASS and drizzle with reserved parsley oil. Serve with carrot stick.

SERVES 1–2

Veggie Power

½ cucumber, peeled and seeded
1 tomato, seeded
½ cup celery, diced
½ cup baby spinach, cut into
    thin strips
1 tbs minced onion
1 cup plain low fat yogurt
Salt
Pepper
Diced yellow bell pepper
    for garnish
Celery sticks for garnish
Celery leaves for garnish

CHOP CUCUMBER and tomato.

IN A BLENDER, combine
vegetables and yogurt and blend
well. Season to taste with salt
and pepper.

POUR INTO A GLASS and
garnish with yellow bell pepper,
celery sticks, and celery leaves.

SERVES 1-2

Vegetable Herb Kefir

1 tbs finely chopped herbs
    (e.g., arugula, basil, parsley,
    celery greens)
½ cup chilled tomato juice
½ cup chilled kefir
½ cup green bell pepper
    flesh, diced
Salt
Pepper
Tabasco Sauce
1 tbs finely diced green bell
    pepper flesh for garnish
Basil leaves for garnish

IN A BLENDER, combine herbs, tomato juice, kefir, bell pepper, salt, pepper and Tabasco, and blend.

CHILL WELL, pour into a glass, and garnish with bell pepper and basil leaves.

SERVES 1–2

TIP

▶ Kefir is produced from cow's milk. A slightly sour brew of fermented milk, kefir is similar in both taste and texture to a liquid yogurt. Many supermarkets carry kefir in the natural food section.

Autumn Smoothie

3½ oz well-chilled cooked
    pumpkin flesh
½ cup well-chilled milk
½ cup well-chilled plain
    low fat yogurt
1 dash vanilla extract
½ cup banana, slightly frozen,
    peeled, and diced
1 pinch cinnamon
1 pinch allspice
1 pinch nutmeg
1 tsp maple syrup
Diced, cooked pumpkin
    flesh for garnish

IN A BLENDER, combine all the
ingredients and blend very well.

POUR INTO A GLASS and
garnish with diced pumpkin.

SERVES 1–2

Cucumber Kefir

½ cucumber
2 tsp lemon juice
1 tbs finely chopped dill
½ cup ice-cold kefir
Salt
Pepper
Cucumber slices for garnish
Dill sprigs for garnish

RINSE, PEEL, seed, and chop
the cucumber.

IN A BLENDER, combine all
the ingredients and blend well.

POUR INTO A GLASS and
garnish with cucumber and dill.

SERVES 1–2

TIP

▶ Kefir is produced from cow's
milk. A slightly sour brew of
fermented milk, kefir is similar
in both taste and texture
to a liquid yogurt. Many
supermarkets carry kefir in
the natural food section.

EXOTIC TASTES

BE ADVENTUROUS AND TRY these recipes for their out-of-the-ordinary flavors. You'll find spicy, bold, and sweet choices to your favorite smoothie combinations. Whether you're blending for your health, cooling down on a warm day, or just trying to put to use fresh vegetables and fruit, smoothies offer an energy boost that will help you achieve optimum nutrition.

Ayran (Turkish Yogurt Drink)

½ cup plain low fat yogurt
Salt
1 dash lemon juice
1 pinch ground cumin
½ cup mineral water
Mint leaves for garnish

BLEND YOGURT, salt, lemon juice, and cumin. Gradually add mineral water, while continuing to blend. Refrigerate for 1 hour.

POUR INTO A GLASS and garnish with mint leaves.

SERVES 1–2

Grasshopper

1 tbs chopped Italian
   parsley leaves
½ cup cold peppermint tea
½ cup plain low fat yogurt
1 dash lemon juice
½ tsp floral honey
1 dash olive oil
Crushed ice
Parsley leaves for garnish
Mint leaves for garnish

IN A BLENDER, combine all
the ingredients except crushed
ice and blend very thoroughly.

PLACE CRUSHED ICE in a glass
and pour drink on top. Garnish
with parsley and mint leaves.

SERVES 1–2

Green Tea Smoothie

½ cup ice-cold green tea
1 cup apricots, slightly frozen,
    pitted, and chopped
½ cup pineapple juice
4 tsp pineapple syrup
½ tsp freshly grated ginger
½ cup mango sorbet
Lemon slices for garnish

IN A BLENDER, combine all the ingredients and blend very well.

POUR INTO A GLASS and garnish with a lemon slice.

SERVES 1–2

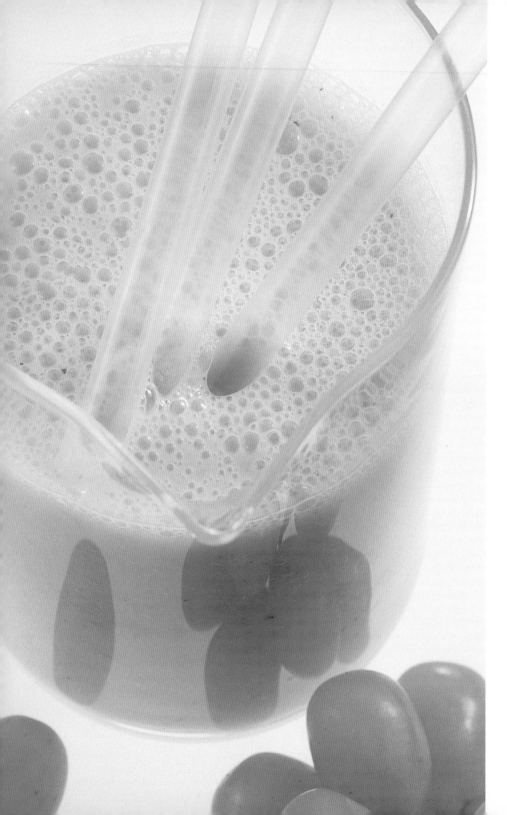

Melon-Grape-Mint Mixer

7 oz honeydew melon flesh
½ lb seedless green grapes
½ cup lemon yogurt
1 tbs lime juice
1 tsp honey
1 tbs finely chopped mint

CHOP FRUIT and freeze slightly.

IN A BLENDER, combine fruit,
yogurt, lime juice, honey and
mint, and blend well.

POUR INTO A GLASS and serve.

SERVES 1–2

Mean Green

½ lb baby spinach, cleaned,
    rinsed, and chopped
½ cup chilled kefir
1 dash lemon juice
Salt
Pepper
Grated nutmeg
2 crushed ice cubes

IN A BLENDER, combine spinach,
kefir, lemon juice, seasonings and
ice, and blend well.

POUR INTO A GLASS and serve.

SERVES 1–2

TIP

▶ Kefir is produced from cow's
milk. A slightly sour brew of
fermented milk, kefir is similar
in both taste and texture
to a liquid yogurt. Many
supermarkets carry kefir in
the natural food section.

Herb Smoothie

2 tbs mixed, fresh, chopped herbs
1 tbs chopped chives
1 tsp mild paprika
Juice from ½ lemon
1 pinch sugar
½ tsp salt
2 tsp grated horseradish
7 drops Tabasco Sauce
1 cup buttermilk
2 cups milk
4 lemon slices for garnish

IN A COCKTAIL SHAKER, mix all the ingredients except the lemon slices and pour into well-chilled glasses.

GARNISH with lemon slices and serve.

SERVES 4

Sultan's Favorite

1 tsp mild Madras curry
1 tsp lemon juice
½ cup banana, slightly frozen,
    peeled, and diced
½ tsp freshly grated ginger
½ cup well-chilled yogurt
½ cup well-chilled milk
Salt
Pepper
A little curry powder for garnish
Several sliced almonds
    for sprinkling

IN A BLENDER, combine all the
ingredients and blend well.

POUR INTO A GLASS, garnish
with curry powder and sprinkle
with almonds.

SERVES 1–2

Herb Buttermilk

½ cup cold buttermilk
2 tsp fresh lime juice
½ tsp grated horseradish
    (from a jar)
2 tbs finely chopped herbs
    (e.g., parsley, chives,
    basil, and dill)
Salt
Coarsely ground pepper
Chives for garnish
Basil leaves for garnish

IN A BLENDER, combine
buttermilk, lime juice,
horseradish, herbs, salt and
pepper, and blend thoroughly.

POUR INTO A GLASS and
sprinkle with chives and coarsely
ground pepper. Garnish with
whole chives and basil leaves.

SERVES 1–2

TOFU ANYONE?

THIS FAVORITE OF THE HEALTH-CONSCIOUS crowd is a hit in smoothies, too! Tofu has a slightly nutty flavor that allows it to take on the flavor of the ingredients it's cooked with. Its texture is smooth and creamy, which provides smoothies with a great consistency. You can find it in most supermarkets and health food stores in regular, low fat, and nonfat varieties.

Silken tofu has a silky-smooth texture and comes in soft, regular, and firm styles (we recommend using soft or regular forms for smoothies).

It's easy to digest, low in calories, calcium and sodium, and high in protein all of which makes it one of today's most healthful food choices.

Tofu Blast

4 oz silken tofu
½ cup well-chilled milk
2 tbs peanut butter
½ cup banana flesh, slightly
    frozen and mashed
1 tsp maple syrup

IN A BLENDER, combine all the
ingredients and blend well.

POUR INTO A GLASS and serve.

SERVES 1–2

Tofruitti

½ cup pineapple flesh, chopped
½ cup banana flesh, chopped
4 oz silken tofu
½ cup pear juice
1 tsp lime juice

CHILL FRUIT very well.

IN A BLENDER, combine fruit,
tofu, pear juice and lime juice,
and blend very well.

POUR INTO A GLASS and serve.

SERVES 1–2

Tofu Zinger

½ cup orange sections, chopped
½ cup banana, peeled and diced
½ medium apple, peeled and diced
4 oz silken tofu
½ cup fresh-squeezed orange juice

FREEZE fruit slightly.

IN A BLENDER, combine fruit,
tofu and orange juice, and blend
very well.

POUR INTO A GLASS and serve.

SERVES 1–2

Asian Smoothie

1 medium nectarine
4 oz silken tofu
½ cup well-chilled mango juice
1 tbs vanilla syrup
1 pinch ginger
Finely diced nectarine flesh
    for garnish

RINSE NECTARINES, cut in
half, remove pits, and chop.

IN A BLENDER, combine all
the ingredients and blend well.

POUR INTO A GLASS and
garnish with nectarine.

SERVES 1–2

INDEX